Brea

Beata Duncan was born in 1921 in Berlin. In January 1934 she and her older brother Tom emigrated to start new lives in England. After the war, she went on to study English Literature at University College London, work in Bloomsbury and initiate her literary career as writer, researcher and tutor. In the early 1970s, she pioneered informal workshops to discuss and edit poetry.

Her gratitude for her refuge in her adopted country, England, and respect for the courage, generosity and compassion she found here, abided and endured till her death in 2015. The peoples and traditions of Britain, her landscape and cities and most importantly her literary culture became the core of her identity.

Berlin Blues, (published in 2017 by Green Bottle Press) describes her first decade in the Weimar period of Berlin.

Breaking Glass recollects her second decade after her arrival in England as a child refugee, the challenge of integration and the English, and her experience as a student during the London Blitz of WWII.

Beata Duncan

Breaking Glass

Vol ii Berlin to London

WriteSideLeft
November 2019

ISBN: Print: 978-1-9161011-4-2
ISBN: eBook: 978-1-9161011-5-9

Compilation & Cover Design by S A Harrison
(text Font design from Bauhaus)
Edited by Stephen Duncan
Photos of Beata Duncan on cover: using contact strip of Beata in
London in c1940—property of Stephen Duncan

Published by WriteSideLeft UK
www.writesideleft.com

For Beata and Tom

Contents

Beata!

I've changed my name,
just the last letter,
the little tail,
from an e to an *a*.

At least the English
might hear, might see
the 'blessed' in Beata,
not think me too 'fancy',

the eternal foreigner,
the visitor, or trip and slip
when they call me
from the queue.

Playground taunts,
the lady in the office,
arching an eyebrow
over the school roll,

even that little thing
might start their stutter,
a cough, with the last
wag of my name.

Better to sing, better
to have the musical lift,
an open *a*
than the threat of an e*!*

Mother-Tongue

A mute until we can arrive, the long
train journey, I refuse to utter German:
to read, to write in my book, never to speak.
I crave English, to be a British girl now!

Can I make the English the present,
leave my German, a tense of the past?
Mouth forming around 'Anglo' sounds,
pushing my lips forward, rounded

to mimic those clipped melodies,
my voice is a different instrument.
A question to be suggested just
with the lift at the tip of my tongue.

It had been the shouting in the street
as I hurried to school that so hurt:
big men with teeth, their horrid words,
schwein, untermensch, to bite me.

Bullies, soldiers, criminals
opening the weapons of their mouths,
a pack of men in their uniforms,
obscenities of their pointing tongues!

Two worlds, two languages, I pass
from one mother to the other: *Victoria please!*
A bus conductor hesitates with my perfect
enunciation. I crave to be the British girl!

My new language step-mothering me,
I will wait many years for soft music—
'liebe, liebling…das ist schoen…' down
a corridor's past, my mother's room…

Other People's Houses

'the children were gone,
the bags were gone,
there was no end-address.'

    Very early, before lessons,
    I watch the dragonfly
    laying eggs, lowering the tip
    of her abdomen into the water,
    a quiver of electric blue
    across the dark pond.

Our dormitory high in the attic,
dormer windows jutting
above the manor house roof,
the boys sleep in the army huts
beyond the neat lawns, the flint wall.

    One night the boys creep
    across the gardens,
    we know they are coming!
    Do I always have to be a 'good sort'?
    Should I be crying?

After tea we have an adventure,
a fire in the woods to warm us,
one cold night and I get all
the blame, I'm asked to leave!

    I always enter
    other people's houses on tiptoe,
    careful of the carpets,
    curious in bedrooms.
    Do I have the right to be here?

Where will I sleep tonight,
where is my cubby-hole?

You pay for it, a disconnect,
the rest of your life.
You find the world
interesting, never *upsetting*.
You choose not to cry.

The dragonfly has laid
her delicate string of eggs,
invisible under the lily leaves.
She hovers above her brood,
flies away on another breeze.

'to do and don't do'

When I arrive the girls see me
as a visitor from another planet,
a foundling without family,
without ancestry or location,

take me carefully into their fold,
vocalising in cautious, well-formed
phrases, as if I might be very good
or very bad, unpredictable.

My new country a formal tribe,
codes of new manners to be learnt,
I keep my hands behind my waist,
each morning a new performance.

Watching for their movements,
a careful mimic of their gestures,
I raise my hand to the mouth,
a napkin wipe, a light cough,

waiting for 'the right moment',
never to brag or show off, confront
or say what you mean, better to say
the opposite, smile and never laugh.

To do and don't do. *Yes* might mean *no*
and *maybe* so necessary, *maybe* and *nice*
will always get me out of a corner,
maybe and nice so useful in a tight spot!

I write in my notebook every night
with the precision of a scientist, revise
and survive without too much bruising.
Until I've 'taken off my shoes'.

A Plum

To be quiet and nice and pretty,
the murmur of new school friends,
the swish of starched white skirts,
I practise a carefully poised smile.

A curl of comportment, a leaf,
might rest on the ledge of my lips.
I walk the school corridor. *Spine,*
spine, never to run or speak out! Rest.

I'm dark and can tan, play tennis,
our 'pluck and pock' song, all day
under the sun. They must shelter
beneath the orchard trees, all fair

and so composed, hold the purple fruit
between forefinger and thumb,
as if this plum will be the only one
they might ever hold in their lives!

I reach up to pick a full, ripe plum,
my hands dripping with the juice,
remembered running home, calling
up the stairs, flipping off my shoes

through the door of her open study
where she would be, arms spread,
her bowl of fruits with purple lights,
a memory still waiting for laughter.

A deep scent of cinnamon, the maternal,
the heavy warmth of her breasts, she had
the certainty of the sun, what it is
to be a woman. She offered me a plum.

I still have my fair friend, her orchard
in the sun, though now in old age we are
as grey and pale as each other.
I'm here, I'm balanced. I hold a plum.

Food Helps

A girl rises to lay the cutlery,
another pours water,
the first days we sit quietly
in rows, dutifully waiting.
Shall I put my hands
under the table, or on top?

I'm puzzled as to the tastes,
the plates served
bland, green and grey.
What I expect to be sour
is sweet, salty neutral,
flavours are difficult to find.

I search inside my mouth,
my memory: pudding little different
to soup, perhaps I could add
the white sugar, the white salt;
always confused, always hungry.
But I'm sprouting!

Nothing can stop my body,
hips and breasts in the quest:
men watch for me
out in the British street.
Periods have started but I already
know what to do.

I can travel up to London
and find another refugee family,
the colour and spice of their meals,
the fast flow, everybody leaning
across the table—excited, passionate,
even with their mouths full!

I find a refugee has dared
to open a delicatessen
in Belsize Park: *Bona*!
A little Berlin on England's Lane!
I can buy a slice of beloved salami,
close my eyes, be home again.

The Girls

Ach! My accent still held
in the throat, too deep, too loud
for the group of friends
I desire, my voice in mime
'breaks' through as it were,
rising so I can be as girly.

I raise the pitch of my voice,
singing in the school choir
until I achieve that sublime note
of virtue, climbing, soaring
every Sunday as a bird
unto the heavens. Crikey!

Strindberg's Grandson

I'm in love with Strindberg's grandson
in my first school in the woods.
He is hesitant, has beautiful dark eyes,
a beautiful dark voice. He understands me.

My bedroom not far from his in the trees;
I don't climb out of the window,
do anything wrong or to be ashamed of.
We are in the deep wood of a dream.

Our headmistress and saviour, Anna Essinger,
has advanced ideas on education,
very free-flowing, very wholesome.
But she doesn't like me, she is a bitch!

She decides we shouldn't see each other,
divides us between two classes, divides us.
I will never see my first boyfriend again
but hope he is happy wherever he is now,

hope he never has to go through anything nasty.
I've always liked his grandfather's plays,
they understand me. I could have been
Miss Julie, he could have been the Father.

He is still in one of my Dream Plays.

The Death of Ophelia

Papa makes some money, writing scripts
for MGM, and says I could be an actress.
At school my best friend's father
Robertson Hare sees my Ophelia,
tells me I should go on the stage.

'I would give you some violets...
they withered all...when my father died'
as I shiver into my paper garlands! I have
a nice figure, I remember the lines, I am her!
He thinks the stream 'particularly fine'.

But every time I try, everyone is busy,
the phone just rings and rings.
I'm passionate enough. Aren't I pretty enough?
So confident and so shy I'll tell you all
what to do and then shut up. I won't be seen.

Papa never speaks about acting again,
he makes no more money. I have to.
But I'll act for you all in my poems,
write the parts, create the roles, seduce you all.
The phone just rings and rings.

The Message

There is a message
I have to collect and run
along the corridor
from study to class,
a school prefect—
a message I had
to collect or pass on,
the proper conduct
of the corridor,
a slow-motion
to hold me back.

There are the
rippling skirts,
the squeak of chalk,
bounce of tennis balls,
a message I leave for you
to collect. I'm returning,
running along the corridor.
Something I forgot to say.
Yes. Will you wait for me?
What can I tell you?

Rising When I'm Falling

Ascending and descending,
the noisy ticket hall of the Underground,

I learn to balance as the escalator
scrolls down in a waterfall of stairs,

balance there above the chrome forest
of lamps, elegant elbow perched

on the moving handrail, the drop
to the tunnels and shelter far below.

I balance past the panels of warnings,
of posters for Kolynos toothpaste, antiseptic,

models so poised in dresses and shoes
I can't afford, in underwear as if we are

all in a state of 'undress', a nakedness
in ourselves, our future. Descending

I look across at the line of strangers
ascending, pass across the message

of a smile, a stare. A silent hymn rising,
falling, I arrive, balanced on the edge.

Part of me rises when I'm falling.

Cable Street

I know Tom has slipped away
to be there, the protest, the Irish.
Heads and arms will be broken,
I remember the marches of Berlin.

The crowds ran as angry ants,
this way and that, reforming,
pushing against, pulling again.
I'm scared he mightn't return.

Will he be hurt? Will he hit?
In Berlin they liked to hurt, to kill.
He will return, dusty and bruised,
a smile, a sigh. I keep supper warm.

The Refugee

He stands up when they play
the National Anthem at the end
of the day, the end of the show,
with just the family there.

I'm now sixteen and grateful
to be released from school
into my new life, the student,
plump, eager, in a new dress.

London is exciting, especially
the Underground with ads
along the escalator: shows,
travel, folk in evening clothes.

I mostly noticed them going up.
Such a steep slope to the bottom,
I'm more concerned going down
to keep my balance.

Dr Israel has a blond moustache,
a blond wreath around his shiny dome,
a distinguished fifty-six, much older
than my father with all his hair.

One of Dr Israel's patients dies,
a woman, it is very unfortunate.
Will he be struck off the register?
there is a lot of furtive talk.

A newspaper, Papa won't tell me.
Engrossed in entrance papers, exams,
dances, boys, I never really know
what happens. Just a refugee.

Moon Coin

When Grandpa sat,
his stomach sat before him.
Across his waistcoat
hung a chain and watch,
I stood close and heard it tick.

He took me to the zoo
on Sunday, we stood close
outside the monkey house
hand in hand. For lunch
he had his own tray

with a lean steak, Granny
and I ate a stew of dumplings,
carrots. A white serviette
tucked into his waistcoat,
he wiped his moustache.

Grandpa liked to hear my bits
of Latin; *Amo, amas* and that.
He smiled like the sun.
I told him about the amoeba
and how it split. He nodded:

'That is how we all began.'
taking a coin from his pocket
as complete and as bright
as the full moon. I spent it on
a lamp for my doll's house.

Wearing a bikini, I sunbathed
on a rock in Cornwall.
Grandpa writes it is no way
for a girl to be photographed.
He dies in the September

of my School Certificate year.
Hot tears rush to my eyes.
My brother has his gold watch.
I can still hear it tick.
There is the moon coin.

Athene's Song

You watched me build the temple,
a broom handle you had cut into columns,
carpenters' wedges for the pediment,
your clever arthritic fingers holding back
until my edifice toppled with a crash

to disturb Grannie's afternoon nap.
You held a finger to your lips
and we began again our build,
the crimson kelim across your study wall
holding us in its attic geometry.

You sang lines from Homer
I couldn't understand, a bird's soft song.
I was to leave you, your gentle calls,
for my own Odyssey to freedom:
the trains and ferry and storms,

my sickness, the fear of drowning,
the fury of the gods. A deliverance,
the 'shipwreck' into a school in Kent,
I found my sheltering cove at a desk,
the night hoot of a little owl, to learn

the Greek, the lines you had sung to me:
the Gatherer of the Clouds sending
Athene of the Flashing Eyes,
'sandals of tarnished gold to carry her
with the speed of wind across the water'.

Deep in my book, not daring to speak,
surrounded by chattering English girls,
their high bird calls, you still come
as my guide, finger to my lips.
I will learn to rise with your song.

The Hill

Why do I have to go to school?
I like the girls but it's all so boring:
exams, common entrance, matric.

I've only to walk up Haverstock Hill
and the tramp devouring schnitzel
will tell me about the great writers,

what they really mean, then tell me
what men and women really need, even
as he tries to look through my clothes.

Soldiers and sailors strolling to the pubs,
a virtuoso violinist playing on the corner,
I can walk up the Hill for a café in the sun,

study Latin with a prize-winning philosopher,
or meet friends at Cosmo—learn
how to make up eyes with soot and cream,

to sew and resew the latest wide trousers,
poach an egg in our upside-down houses
when all our lives homes had servants.

Walking up the Hill for the sunny Heath
I was the dark beauty and a young poet
wrote a complete book of poems about me.

I have them now in a grey-card wallet
he made from a cardboard cartridge case.
I know books are more dangerous

than bombs or the Blitz and hide them away.
I haven't opened them, I haven't pulled the pin.
I know they will go off like a grenade.

The Seaside

To the seaside for an ice cream,
an easy hitch with all the lorry traffic,
to hear, to smell the sea, the coming storm.

I sit with my older brother in the sun.
We are old enough not to be with our parents,
young enough to worry where they are.

A boy in a uniform patrols the prom,
stops us from bathing. Oh thank God
for the Channel, the refreshing British sea!

The high waves roll in from another land,
tides of barbed wire staked across the beach.
A dark, boarded-up hotel, men are mixing cement.

The signals of seagulls, a sea of breakers
bring a current of messages, a code of murmuring.
We listen. We are very quiet.

Troikas

I want to help, please,
with the refugees, always
coming in threes.

A thump and rattle,
I complete the course, touch-type
as fast as a drummer, a machine.

Bitte Setzen! Forms must have
their copies, I'll list you all
in triplicate! Three teas!

I type asleep in the office,
fall awake in the basement shelter,
fingers waltzing in threes.

The clatter of typewriters,
punctuation, dreams punctuated
by sirens, the knock of knees.

Three gloves, three socks,
three hats, I'll see you
in thirds, trios, triplets.

Dance with me, dance with me
down the aisle of steel desks,
a troika of threes!

The Grand

It was a madness,
everyone in the street
leaving for the country,
leaving emptied houses,
a feast of furniture
out on the pavement
for our choice!

A Grand Piano,
Collards of Camden Town,
I walk around it,
know I have to have it!
A promise of a meal,
friends pull it up the steps
into the empty front room.
I don't need anything else—
sleep under it, live with it,
play it!

A deep black lacquer,
the great lid raised,
the harp inside waits for my fingers.
Practise, practise.
Just a girl, stretching
my arms, my hands
the deep sound overwhelms me.
To play all through the noise,
create my own thunder,
songs to muffle noisy nights.

Standing in my room,
waiting for me to open and play,
allow it to speak, to sing,
I return home each day,
faithful to my love,
full of song.

My fingers itching
to span, to flex, to strike,
to press the keys *pianissimo*!
In the silence, the strings
continue to sing.

Wrapped in a bed
of thick quilts
I lie under it,
strings thrumming
with the planes above.
Play me, play me!

My Wolves

They take the animals away, a convoy
of calls, an exodus, an ark from the Zoo,
trucks and trains leaving for the country,
along with the children, the evacuees.

When the artillerymen cut down the trees
to bare the crown of lovely Primrose Hill,
I hear the howls of the wolves left behind,
with the sirens before the bombs will fall.

Their cries leaping the railway line, the Hill,
streets of bricks and branches and shrapnel,
find me as I hear the sirens, another howl,
a refuge with a refugee, howls curling with me.

The howls take me to the Tiergarten trees,
back to the Zoo of my Berlin, to my family
of wolves loping the line of their wire.
They will howl too when the bombs fall.

Grey ears and golden eyes, I felt their call.
We would stand and hold our level gaze,
my bare, cold knees below my skirt,
thin legs and tendons beneath their fur.

Eye to eye either side of the long wire,
we gaze at each other still. They will howl
when the bombs fall on London, on Berlin.
We will all howl and howl when they fall.

To Be Important

they repeat the same argument,
they argue about the same thing,
as if they cannot do anything but argue
until in boredom I begin knitting again.

Their words will be in a new sweater:
plain and purl, yes and no, right or wrong,
left and right, rich and poor, dos and don'ts;
with the knitting mother taught me.

In the boarding house, by the fire,
pulling a lump of yarn from my bag,
I feel mother through the thread of wool,
another line as a thread to the past.

How she held my fingers from behind,
guiding the angle of needles,
the tightness of the yarn,
how to slip one over the other,

loop and dip and pull. I knit
with her hands, my sweater with
her sounds in the pattern—
put your lips close, you can feel

the texture of voices, the warm breath
of mother close behind. I knit
with her hands, a rhythm to the past.
A *masterpiece* they all tell me.

'Potato Pete'

You arrive with a tin of whale meat
in your arms! Oh Blubber, oh love!
                          Oh so sweet!
Not hard to keep trim the ration years,
pretend a parsnip can be a vol-au-vent!

Mashed potato twirled into a palace
of all the fantasies the Ministry tells.

To fool ourselves, I hoarded a packet
of dried bananas, so black, so sweet!

You slip your arm around my waist,
'Captain Carrot' and 'Potato Pete'.
 Oh Blubber, oh love! Oh so sweet!

The Philosopher

I've fallen in love with a philosopher!
What a fool I am, what a nightmare,
he so much older. I listen intently
to his interpretations of Hegel,
his analysis of the War, the inevitable
progress of history, of our lives!
It is so erotic: his dark Marxist beard,
a professorial pause, his eyes.
I hold my breath in the deep silence
while he thinks. Oh darling, I'm so
excited by the power of his brain.
When he looks at me
I'm the only little genius alive!

The Physicist

A luminous man, my brother's friend,
we had known him a long time
when he came to share our flat.
Entering rooms of shadow, speaking late,
they were intoxicated with a world
of intricacies I would always be outside.
Air thick with plumes they smoked new pipes,
a whistling suck of stems, gurgles,
in the pause of low earnest words.

We had made a new family for him,
giving me the photos of his Berlin childhood,
trusting us with those he had lost.
We were all lost but trying together to find
our way. Yes, I loved him back, his wide
Oxford trousers, bitten stems rising
from the top pocket of old tweeds,
hidden lumps of inky pens, thick notebooks
with the energy of calculations, logarithms!

What is *matter*? What are these particles
dancing beyond the surface of appearance?
How can you be certain by equation?
What of the energy of things? It was sunlight
warming a room that touched me, how the rays
slid from one side of a room to the other,
turning it inside out by the end of the day.
I know it nearly killed him, my cruelty,
the rejection. I carry the story with me.

It Is

a scent in the room
a sneeze in a dusty breeze
clothes that are damp
it is a kiss

a crumbling house
the complete black-out
whispers are my guide
it is a kiss

it is as simple
as a loaf of bread
our rations of cheese
it is a kiss

a call in the night
an owl and a strike
a blow that never comes
it is a kiss

a siren from the Hill
the ack-ack of a great gun
the deep grind of lorries
it is a kiss

a farewell overheard
a couple who can't let go
your arrival and farewell
it is our kiss

A Perfume Bottle

Antelope, Tresor, Magie,
Emeraude, Marrakech,

I look into the bottles,
the remaining amber liquor
a slow gold in the bottom
of the last, as far away
as I am now from there,
still as intense,
its remaining sweetness
as powerful as I remember,
the heady honey vapour,
the hint of musk, a spice
out of the Bible.

I have been given
a tiny bottle, cut glass sides
of diamonds, a stopper as round
as the roof of a mosque,
tight with a turn,
the secret essence of a stink,
I can lift the stopper in private
and breathe!

I know it has been carried
by a caravan of camels,
ornate glass curves
the swags of a tent,
scents from the East,
precious frankincense
and myrrh.

I have
a silver box
for a secret cream,

an enamelling
of camels under stars,
a round powder pack
with a secret powder,
a secret waxy stick of pink
that hasn't yet moulded
to my lips.
A new adventure.
I am a girl.

Learning to Powder

The comforting scent of rosewater,
a sweetness, I learn to powder,
my first shade of Suntan (by Ponds),
my first handbag with a lipstick.

Easing open the lid without a spill,
I tuck back a curl, brush my cheek
with the powder puff, a wisp of the dust
in the breeze. I walk up the Hill,

turn into the shelter of a doorway,
a shop window, a cinema foyer—
learn to powder with the sways of a bus!
Bombed buildings grey in the rains,

a dark river of silt and brick
covers the stink of lives, until the sun
dries it all, loose dust rising again
along the High street, the Hill.

Passing the damp snout of sandbags,
the entrance to the Tube of Belsize Park
I'll go on to Cosmo for real coffee, no chicory,
If I can afford a slice of Sachertorte!

A pink powder, my 'bronze' shade,
rises before I reach the café,
a skirl of wind to lift my skirt.
I powder my nose. I walk up the Hill.

The King

I learn never to hesitate,
never hesitate to stand straight,

before the newsreels start,
before the bobbing of ships,

the flicker of distant men.
There will be the ricochet

of folding cinema seats,
loud as a round of gunfire,

when the anthem is played,
hands down, face up for the King.

The Offcuts

Drowsy with the sweet balsamic fumes,
rabbit-skin glue warming on a flame,
a low shivering light around the kitchen table,
we make rows of wooden toys for 'the war effort',
lost in the late nights, lost in the year of '42.

Offcuts from the munition factories, the waste
from turning machines, cutters and guillotines,
boxes of these elemental shapes are 'the good design',
an art-school exercise someone has remembered,
Bauhaus principles of circle and triangle and square.

'How are we to live well together'*— be sensible,
no crying, sentiment or grief: a train, a boat, a lorry,
we pin and screw and joint the toys together
from these offcuts— a nailing of blows, a jolly painting
with the bright red and yellow and blue?

A thick coal dust from the glimmering fire,
a reek of paraffin from the murmuring stove,
how can we just give the children these offcuts
from munitions, the boxes from bullets, the crates
for bombs? And who is going to stir the stew?

A world of good faith, even if the roofs fall in,
if a campaign fails there will always be the new.
Cut off from the old country we are all offcuts,
discarded shapes, waiting to see what we could
make of ourselves, the red and yellow and blue.

Offcuts will see us through until we can begin again,
clear the rubble, build something new.
The War cuts us all, deeply, but I know
what it is to be wounded, without the saw's nick,
without the red and yellow and blue.

*Walter Gropius, founder of the Bauhaus design school.

Careless

Never gossip about your work,
never complain of a failure
or boast of a success, never say
what you have just done

or what you will do, never
explain where you go or
will be, never ask a direction
when the road names and signs

are down, the lights are out.
Just wait at the crossroads.
After all, if you don't know
the turnings, who might you be?

Just listen to the radio, a band,
a cookery or comedy show.
Just meet me at the cinema—
find each other, be close.

Just talk of the loves
and lives of the film stars,
just gaze into the light
and dark of the screen.

The Sausage

At first it might seem not so bad
in the old country: some return,
unhappy in exile. But we are young,
enough to make a home here
of our new refuge, to work and study,
even during the fears of invasion.

We can take it. There are the jokes:
What does a German abroad say
to another? Are you a Jew too?
The dangerous jokes: a Berlin circus
trains its chimps the silly salute,
to raise an arm at every uniform.

But after the 'night of broken glass'
we know how cruel they will be.
Their new laws to make us into victims.
That ridiculous man in a moustache
and fantasy uniforms started shouting
'You won't be laughing any more!'

Sirens every night, planes above,
can I be trained, learn to fire a gun?
I collect knives, thrust at the mirror.
It was a sausage bought in a corner shop
that makes me smile, all I can afford
for my brother and me, alone in this flat.

I'll always like a sausage, even the ones
for the ration, full of gristle and marrow!
I'll cut it in half and watch the fat
flow out as it fries. We're determined
to survive, if they come we both agree
we will kill. Oh for the British 'banger'!

Tyrannos

Your face is always there,
the heavy jowl, the floppy lock of hair,
a comedian's moustache! The uniforms!

It is personal, the newsreels
and jeers in the cinema, the Tommies
singing about your 'one ball'.

It's personal all through the war,
a tyrant ruling without law—
we knew you would, to do your worst.

You play the devil, all your costumes
as in a theatre. You are the devil,
a divine mission to destroy and devour.

It's personal, you boast you have a list,
will know my name and where I live,
know I've escaped.

It's personal, your mechanical strut,
goosestepping across the Channel
if we ever give in or give up.

It's personal, to fight your mad eyes
in their dark shadows, the open rant
that you want to exterminate me.

It's personal like a duel. Hate and fear
are the combatants. But I know you
are already an old man, and I am young.

Goethe

We are a home of 'intellectuals', far, far
from *the land where the lemon trees bloom,*
students in our teens when the Blitz begins,
everyone leaving the city, a flat easy to find.

Tom invites me to share a 'palace' with a pot
and pan, the days the bombs began to fall.
Empty rooms, an overgrown garden without end,
I lay my single mattress on the floor.

A splintered kitchen table to shelter under,
the thick fabric of blackout curtains
(the 'Victorian funeral skirt') to shut us in,
we all work through the night on our revision.

The fever of exams, a boy in love with me,
we are called the 'red house': there was Marx
and the socialism we lived for, '1840 and 1940',
the class struggle, making toys with scraps of wood.

Little jobs for £2 per week, a philosopher
Wields a hammer, a poet a paintbrush.
I become an expert with a touch of pink
for the doll's cheek, a dash of *lippy* for my lips.

Revising notes for The Wars Of The Roses
as the sirens go off, we sing out *Oh my god
not again.* To be dead is one thing, alive another.
Only with the danger of death, a house with a corpse,

can we understand a philosophy of the living:
to study for every moment of our lives!
A gleaning of old books, science and history,
the German stack, an English pile, Poetry,

someone rich and absurd lent us a complete suite
of Goethe's furniture, reproductions from Weimar-
a quartet of elegant empire chairs, a dining table,
a collection of his novels—until 'we are back'.

Refusing to take cover during the raids, lying
on the pretty velvet couch with his *The Sorrows
Of Young Werther* for his darling Lotte,
I read by the arrows of moonlight

falling through the criss-cross of taped windows.
A boy in love with me. I read and reread
Goethe's letter to Ackerman: *'this creation...
I fed with the blood of my own heart.'*

Beethoven

I need your sustenance, to work and study
without sleep, the nightly bombs
and grief, stifled by dusty blackout curtains,
without street lights or the stars.
I'll need the touch of your sounds again.

A candle by the radio, I crouch close,
the thrill of the broadcasts for the BBC,
the victory V in your Symphony 5,
the drum-roll motif to Europe,
the low 'bom, bom, bom, boom'.

I lie on the floor and receive you,
play again the old Busch 'Berlin' records
I was given by a frightened evacuee,
the relentless rhythm of restless strings
in the excitement, the intimacy of their play.

Discs of Toscanini and your Pastoral,
soaring notes of gentle woodwind,
a flight of notes climb high as swallows,
all know their place in the orchestral flock,
know the intervals, high in their murder.

In the total noise of a raid I can follow
your new road in the Sixth, the great river
of rhythms, to be in the enfolding flood,
your surge of strings, moving as a swimmer
swept forward in the torrent of your creation,

or come through the thunder to rest
in the clear sunlight, the storm's other side,
to be washed clean by your rain,
trust in you as the 'good German',
rest again in your open arms.

A Coat

A belt, a trilby hat,
nap still clogged
with a film of soot,
crockery wrapped
in shirts, books by vests,
jewellery is laid in a pair
of knickers. I spot
the lovely tweed coat

across a kitchen table
on the pavement before
the injured, blackened house,
casualties taken to the 'stations'.
Something cheap
after the raids,
the street 'bomb sales'
from those who will not return,

it will be a thick check
for me and the winter.
A faint salty, smoky scent,
no matter the cologne
I spill on the collar,
no matter my warmth
after a night out,
I want to wear my coat.

If I have a row
with someone I love,
there will be the wail—
the sirens, the rush
to hide, the bang.
There will be bodies.
They'll wander
through the night,
looking for their clothes.

Top Secret

I

You were a brilliant boy, so brainy, so sporty—
our whole family had whispered 'wunderkind'!
Learning English fast, your degree a year early,

it felt like an athlete's race—whenever I caught up
you had hurtled on. I would always have to run fast
those insane years together, without parents.

I chose to read British Constitutional History
when it was time. I struggled so, must have been mad!
Reserved for 'work of national importance',

you weren't transported to the Isle Of Man,
interned behind rolls of barbed wire, an enemy alien.
After the interview with Watson-Watt

(guarded by a Tommy), the top-secret work
you refused to explain absorbed you, drowned you:
a sea of cryptic diagrams, numbers and questions,

as I left out a supper tray for those late nights;
locked cupboards, boxes of valves bristling
with fine insect filaments inside their glass nipples.

Perfect circles rose steadily in a column
from your new pipe, through all the turbulence
of the raids. Dark circles around your eyes.

2

I've finally overtaken you. A scientist true
to your faith you had insisted on cremation,
to be scattered at sea, restless ashes

in the circling of a slow, reluctant current.
I think of you on a ship in a war film,
a green blip on a trembling screen,

radio waves of radar, their repeating circles
moving you slowly towards the horizon edge.
You disappear from us into the other side,

to where you have taken an oath of secrecy,
can never tell us what you will have found.

Upstairs

upstairs the bars of the balustrade
climb to the pale sun of the skylight

upstairs and the long empty rooms
we should not enter live by themselves

upstairs a piano wrapped in a dust sheet
hums with a harp of strings

upstairs where the electrics have been cut
and only the moonlight walks

upstairs where the empty rooms
echo with the drone of planes

on clear starry nights
upstairs where I have never climbed

downstairs sheltering in the basement
an overgrown garden a deep green light

Fireworks

I can't return to the Underground,
its dirty brown tiles, wet sandbag walls,
take shelter with all the rest,
the sweaty and crying, the waiting
for the worst to come and be gone,

even if I do learn a new game of cards.
I don't want to sleep the night
in the garden shelter with Tom,
filling with water the last time
we had a storm, whining mosquitoes

above my bunk like a circle of planes,
and wait for the siren. I don't want to
lie under the kitchen table, watching
the boards vibrate as I twist and turn
on the fold-out army bed. I'll climb

to the top of our deserted house,
open the blackout, watch it all in the dark,
an armchair in front of the open window,
as in a cinema. I can still see the film:
the flaming gun on Primrose Hill,

the *ach ach ach* of its great bird call,
the bangs and probing lights to catch
heavy bellies flying in-and-out of cloud;
the high wolf-whistle of a falling bomb,
tense rows of houses, hunched in the dark.

Fires along the railway line lighting up
the sky, showers of sparks for a hit,
a saucepan floating above the gardens,
each blast sends its thump into my chest,
squeezing me into the chair. I gasp for breath.

Holding a stunned bird in my hands,
a cage of fingers, warm and fluttery
until it recovers, I can feel the strength
of feathers bracing my fingers,
an explosion of wings as it bursts, rising.

'Cupateadarlin'

Just a girl, standing guard, taking 'speed' to keep awake,
I keep up and get through exams, write essays by a torch-
beam,

listen for the air-raid howls, my next watch of the roofs,
working hard at my study of Elizabeth's Albion.

Her dark tensions and fears of invasion, *the Virgin Queen's*
secret police, I paint toys in a neighbour's kitchen workshop,

run errands for the refugee committee, a student dance,
walk to lectures at Birkbeck through the black-out,

a warden shouting at me as I slip past. To fight in the dark.
A multitude of uniforms carry holsters, the weight of guns,

I know all those who have them will want to use them.
I love my new city, her great doors and silhouettes,

feel my way to Gower Street for meetings of College Council,
my fingers spread to touch pitted stone and sooted trees,

the silky skin of a barrage balloon, sinking for lack of air or gas,
a silver creature pulsing above the traffic of the Euston Road.

The duck of a torch, shiver of a flame with the shuddering air,
there will be the song of a 'cupatea?', a copper urn appearing

after every bang. I'll wade through streets of shattered glass,
a man leaning at the corner, skin covered in thorns of blood.

Shepherded from casualties by the arms of strangers,
I don't want to see the 'bits' along the curb, soft floppy forms

laid out on stretchers, the burnt-out eyes of a piano factory
at Camden Town. The jazz band plays in a basement,

a spiv calls from a doorway, a spy waits in a lounge,
you know your friends the way silhouettes move,

you can tell who you might fear the way they stand still.
By day the police direct everyone, by night are secret again.

Breaking Glass

The thugs *breaking glass* seem to follow me
after that terrible night, vibrations of their loathing
when the Blitz finally begins, as if they know me,
blasts to break the glass, blow in my windows.

In the *all-clear* I find a perfect glass vase
in a junk shop on the Camden Road: an elegant neck,
a handle curved to the base, the belly a water drop
the sunlight fills, passing through.

Poised on the mantlepiece, empty or with flowers,
it will survive for *the duration*, a precious talisman
I will too. But even now the sound of windows
breaking will upset me, a threat, an anxiety.

Those pieces of window glass will trigger
a pain in my fingers, a quiver in my stomach.
I'll muffle the fragments in newspaper,
a package as a rite, before the sickness arrives.

My glass vase like a beautiful bomb, I'm jittery
in case it explodes and all will be over.
Despite my famous clumsiness I have it still,
poised on top of the bookcase, a delicate perfection.

Abschied

The place for exotic sandwiches,
fillings of dates and cream cheese, real coffee,

the great galleries emptied of their paintings,
the Tommies lie on the floor before the piano

as she plays, boys closing eyes for the prelude,
soldiers with wet cheeks as she begins the etude

searching for a shape, towards a resolution.
The slow notes, the deep sounds

entering them, searching for their feeling,
gives a moment to be retained, remembered,

her concert grand a great chest of strings,
a sonata sonorous in the trembling chests of men.

Waiting for the end, the embarkation, the leave,
this is their room, listening to German music,

living this moment until the whistles, the drop of flags:
Adieu, Abschied, Farewell,

the station the other side of the square of Generals,
the lines of impatient trains.

Buck Up

For six years I refuse to cry,
not once, the 'stiff upper lip'
gets us through.

Streets of rubble,
restless soldiers and sailors,
woman driving, leading,

winters won't stop us,
queuing at hospitals
to give blood.

Even when it is just
a meal a day we say the pie
is so good this week,

even if it is all gristle
under a baroque crust,
the cake full of chalk.

Even if clothes run out
I patch and repatch the inside,
hiding the tear, our terror.

If you are anxious,
fear you have lost someone,
does it matter?

Everyone has,
you aren't special.
I lost the hang of it,

the gift of tears.
It took a very long time.
Finally I got it back.

By Air

Your letters on such thin blue
airmail paper are a tissue as light

as a breeze, the flow of weather,
a slight weight as precious as gold,

a gold leaf for me, a gilding of clouds,
on their flight from you!

The paper becomes so transparent,
your sloping pen, words both sides,

ink seeping through, appear from behind.
And you are with me again, here and now,

arms around me, your sigh
and smile and concentration to form

a doubled message in overlap, loops
of urgent, unutterable embraces.

A Bitterness of Temper

Sipping your smoky English tea,
you took it black and bitter, enjoying
a blend from complementary estates,
solvent awhile with new film scripts.

Papa, you might be in court before us,
judge and jury, eloquently skilled
to justify your actions— this time
what you did to mother, your wife.

What you couldn't do, wouldn't do
to help her—helpless, alone, isolated
in Berlin boarding houses, the limbo
of a lingering divorce while you flew,

intoxicated with your power,
a magnet for actresses, scented women,
in the prowl of your emigration:
opening nights of Vienna, Paris, London.

Ah, but you were a trained advocate,
a doctor of law, of jurisprudence,
knew how to defend yourself,
with your pugilistic sport,

boxing your way out of every corner—
defend yourself against the ropes,
any attack of responsibility, shame,
the selfishness of need, desire.

Standing up for yourself
as bright and clean as virtue:
'what could one do?' you shrug.
Mother sank without trace.

As bright as 'the playwright'
always with the right words
for your characters, dialogue
just rolling from you,

the reasonable words of justification:
history governs our actions,
the dilemmas 'life throws at one',
I would put you in court again.

Acrimony. My Oxford definition gives
a bitterness of temper,
that unique blend of anger, guilt, grief.

.

Milk

Rooms of grey walls and an iron bed,
the monotones of brown food, soup,
the lid of a bill covering a glass of milk
for your next precious cup of coffee,
quivered from the bomb blasts.

Brick dust sifting from the cracks
onto your papers, clothes, the cup:
Father, what were you writing
in those Paddington boarding houses,
so important' in your exile?

The Tyrannos essay for your Club 43,
there was your war of words, scripts
for the radio, the BBC, the US Army,
'what Germany might be after the War',
propaganda broadcasts back to Berlin,

drug-addled Goebbels with vulpine eyes
watching his favourite romantic films,
unaware the scripts had been by you:
one of your many pseudonyms of course,
to have made money, sustain a career.

A dust floating on the white milk
of their racist madness, your weapon
against the tyrant, a restless quiver of pens,
arrows at the 'pure and German',
they lapped from the drink you gave them.

Cruel and kind, you had always played
for us the roles of your characters,
an entertainment. Did I ever have the real you?
How clean does a glass of milk have to be?
Dust breathes from the cracks in the wall.

Summer Sonata

Practising the difficult, the late 110,
you would stick on the same phrase
stopping and starting, to begin again,
an insect in the well-oiled machine,
a zip catching on a hem, a sticking door,

a fly bumping against the window,
fingers colliding, a mind tripping over,
a silent cry as I bent to my homework,
tension tightening, the coming of thunder,
the collision of clouds, the struggle.

You insisted on practice before supper
while the sun played out in the garden
beyond the open window and I knew
what work this was, the anxiety,
I knew your summer hay scent of sweat,

fingers slipping on and off the keys,
how the 110 was really too hard for you,
the repeated phrase in your far-off study
now come to fill again the vestibule,
as I tried to finish my assignments,

keys quickly thumping their hammers,
rows of vibrating wires in the machine
within, the cavern of heavy wood and steel
and dust, the black polished piano beast,
a tyrant, until the Beethoven flows again

in the way the sun draws the moisture
from the hay, the sweetness rising,
nothing will be born without practice,
without the pain and warmth of desire,
the sun, I remember you say, play

the questioning note after the storm…
you talk to me, the repeated question
of perfection, of how to play, to practise
as I sit and listen now in the concert hall…
the soloist flowing, the notes rising…

What Happened to the Toys?

The friends of my first decade,
there was the poodle on wheels,
my *pudel*, her fur to my cheek,
her back of curly black wool
I could sit astride.

There was the American doll
I had called Gladys, her smile
and box of silk dresses.
Oh the giraffe, whose long neck
could watch over my shoulder!

The toys! Were they all arrested
and locked in a box? Did they
have their clothes taken away?
Were they put in an oven,
thrown into a fire? What happened?

Starving Myself

When I thought you couldn't,
I stopped eating so that I could hope,
hope you might eat.

I never knew how much food you had
(in hiding, on the run, the arrest...)
despite your last reassuring letter.

I could feel how thin the air-mail paper,
how thin you might be. Safe here in London,
I never knew anyone who was fat.

It wasn't difficult with our rations,
all elegantly thin in service trousers
or dresses cleverly repaired, taken in.

After the war there were the years
of telegrams, letters searching for you,
the Red Cross, the CTB, the US Army!

I had to accept you had been starved,
killed, you hadn't survived.
I knew I had to survive, try to eat,

gain again the weight.
Can I have what you lost?
Mother, let me live again.

Gin

When I grow tired of the stuffy air, the smell,
the crying and rustling of a little hell,

when I grow tired of those shelters Underground,
the endless bombs and Jerry's 'round',

when I'm fed up with the Duties, their Frown,
I can walk away to Camden Town.

The music halls, the Old Bedford, the Camden, the Park,
I'll sit high in their warm naughty dark,

the magic row of uplights for the cave of the stage,
enjoy silly songs 'all the rage'.

I'll look down on the little fat man in a tartan cap,
looking up with his finger to his lip,

stretching his braces with a click and a clink.
He'll sing and sigh 'here's a wink':

*'Don't tell my mother I'm living in sin,
don't let the old folks know!*

*Don't tell my brother I breakfast on gin.
He'd never survive the blow.'**

Oh when I'm tired I can sing this song of sin,
longing for the end, the win, the gin!

*A.P Herbert

The Girl

A girl is running towards me,
follows a ball along the corridor
of shadows, high dark ceilings,
the moulding's plaster foliage.

She has my face, my eyes,
passing by, a deluge of light
from the courtyard beyond.
I don't want to look anymore.

Afterword by Stephen Duncan

In January 2015, a few months before she died, my mother Beata Duncan asked me to edit and organise her unpublished poetry for collections and submissions to publishers. I accepted her request, knowing the quality of her work and having worked closely with her on the editing of it for many years, becoming familiar with the nature of her own creative process: her subject matter and language, line length and rhythm, the organisation and edit of stanzas.

After her death I faced the challenge of the volume of work she had left: stacks of boxes with varied drafts and notes as well as her notebooks, a sometimes confusing sequence. I have tried to organise and collate, relive my mother's creativity, sustain her voice and acknowledge the tough editorial standards she always set herself.

It was clear to me that Beata's poetry could fall into a narrative of time, the subsequent decades of her life, with enough poetry to make a sequence of collections beginning with *Berlin Blues* (published in 2017 by the Green Bottle Press) describing her first decade in the Weimar period of Berlin, the city of her birth.

This subsequent collection, *Breaking Glass*, is formed from an equal number of poems describing her second decade after her arrival in England as a child refugee, the challenge of British life and her gradual integration, and her experience as a student during the London Blitz of World War II.

With the events of those war-time years and the difficulty of expressing that experience after a long period of suppression, the poetry of *Breaking Glass* was largely (as with *Berlin Blues*) written in Beata's last decades and was part of a late creative release.

Much of *Breaking Glass* is in the present tense as if to engage the reader in the immediate experience of a young woman during the dramatic events of her early years, an experience of memory spanning more than half a century. She seemed to have reached a period where she needed to

73

recover these memories, perhaps as a way of completing her life: a writing approach with the power of a creative memory, a fusion of memoir and documentation with the intensity of a poet's emotional language.

Further developments for her poetry have been the interest of several composers and singers in compositions of her poems as song cycles and cabarets, including the composers Richard Arnell and Andreas Demetriou, creative echoes of the music and theatre of the early Weimar years in Berlin. Current collaborations with Demetriou and the Berlin Blues Cabaret has created a new world of music and performance that would have delighted Beata.

Additional published and unpublished poetry describes her post-war life as a single-parent after the early death of my father Adrian, her working life as a researcher, librarian and tutor and her own literary research, writings and 'observations' of her grandchildren.

Beata went on to read, broadcast and publish her poetry with several prizes throughout her long life and was a popular performer of her work in north London.

After their father left Germany in 1933 the family had to move from their parental home in Berlin to their grandmother Agnes Stadthagen's smaller apartment nearby. This accommodation was limiting and claustrophobic and Beata's brother Tom in particular pushed for their emigration, only too aware of the increased proscriptions and legal changes that were already applied by the new German government, the threatening future to Germans of Jewish origin.

The decision to emigrate was also propelled by the political position of their father, the playwright Hans Rehfisch, who was known for his anti-Nazi views. He had been included on the Nazi list of banned writers and several of his theatre productions had been mobbed by right-wing gangs. Arrested in March of 1933, months after Hitler came to power, he was released on condition he immediately left Germany, leaving for Austria and Vienna where he had a play in production. Hans continued his career in the theatres of Vienna and Paris until he finally arrived in London in 1936, initially to work on film scripts for the British film industry.

Tom's and Beata's parents had become estranged, their marriage to end in divorce.

Their mother Lilli remained in Germany in close proximity to her remaining family and relatives and her father-in-law, the physician Eugen Rehfisch. She was known for her practice as an Adlerian therapist (including work with the Institute For Individual Psychology in Berlin, the centre for therapists following its founder Alfred Adler), articles and radio talks and collaboration with her mentor, the Adlerian therapist and philosopher Alexander Neuer. She continued to communicate by letter to her children in England (via relatives in the USA after the outbreak of WW II) until her arrest and deportation to a concentration camp in late 1941 where she was to perish.

On their arrival in England, Beata and her older brother Tom attended the Bunce Court School for refugee children in

Kent, a school that was to give both children a focus for their new lives. This German-speaking school, run by the visionary teacher Anna Essinger, was a relocation of her school from Herllingen in Germany in 1933 and was run along progressive lines with an emphasis on the arts, self-sufficiency and exercise. A remarkable group of children came to find sanctuary at Bunce Court, including the film-maker Peter Morley and the artist Frank Auerbach. An exceptional person of energy and resolution, Essinger expanded her work, after the events of Kristallnacht in 1938, organising schools for the many refugee children needing support with the Kindertransports out of Nazi-occupied Europe.

Both of the children soon left Bunce Court School, Tom after a year to train as an engineer, eventually graduating with a BSc degree in Electrical Engineering from the University Of London. Beata as a rebellious spirit did not get on with Essinger; she wanted to be within an English-speaking community with her ambitions for a university studentship and after a second year went on to a more conventional school.

Although Beata had been learning English in Berlin before emigration (and quickly became proficient in the language) the first poems in this collection *Breaking Glass* witness the difficulties of adapting to English conventions and the mystery, the subtlety of manners she found in her subsequent school and institutions. After this difficult time she made life-long friends with several English girls, friendships that helped her to assimilate with her new country, perhaps allaying the increasing concerns for her mother and family remaining in Germany.

Both Tom and Beata were registered under the Aliens Registration Act at the outbreak of WW II despite their refugee status. Tom with his talents and training in engineering and maths was exempt from the Internment in 1940 of all males from Germany or Austria, as he had employment with key companies for the war-effort on 'work of national importance'. He spoke little of this employment, no doubt bound by the Official Secrets Act, but it seems to have involved a contribution to developments in electronics, radio and radar and eventually to have lead to his post-war research.

Hans lived separately from his children in north London, had initially on his arrival in the UK written film scripts, had several of his plays in production and was able, at first, to offer some financial assistance to Beata. While she was of average academic abilities Beata had drive and purpose, working hard throughout the trauma of the War to educate herself and pass exams, in addition to serving on University Committees as the 'refugee' representative. She described to me taking stimulants including barbiturates to get through the night in her effort to absorb so much academic information, after working all day and with little sleep due to the air raids.

This began a remarkable period of their lives, a community of refugees with an extraordinary range of creative abilities, talents and experience, residing particularly in the Camden Town, Belsize Park, and West Hampstead areas of North London.

After her school years, Beata came to live in a series of boarding houses in north London until the outbreak of World War II, eventually sharing a flat in the 1940s with her brother Tom in Belsize Park. With the threat of mass bombing of the city, empty flats for rent had become available after the evacuation of many families, often leaving furniture behind to be 'borrowed' by those who remained. Despite their relative poverty, Tom and Beata were able to live with some space and basic style, improvising with a 'make-do and mend' confidence. Beata enrolled as a BA student to study History at Birkbeck College, part of the University Of London that allowed students to study in the evenings. She could be employed during the day with a succession of part-time jobs, including domestic labour, a workshop making toys and even briefly, acting as nanny to Churchill's grandchildren in the home of the Government Minister, Duncan Sandys.

With their left-wing heritage, their home was known as 'the red house' by their friends, a community of young people, largely without parents or family, who shared their determination to get through the war, find employment and make their contribution to society and the future. Beata probably encountered as many stimulating people as she would have done in Berlin, though now with the added edge of the war, danger and the continuous threat of invasion and bombing. They remained in their Belsize Park homes all through the Blitz, sheltering in the Belsize Park Underground Station, the 'Anderson' bomb shelter in their garden or sleeping under the kitchen table or even, as she describes, taking the risks of witnessing the bombing and destruction from the top-flat windows.

The ordeal of the war was eased by the vicinity of Hampstead Heath and the chance of relaxing with friends by the ponds and hills overlooking the city, a haven of countryside so important to their world.

The central poems of this collection account for this period and its effects on their lives. The group of poems, *The Grand Piano, Beethoven, Abschied, Gin,* celebrate moments of wartime culture and entertainment. While the artworks that had been installed in the National Gallery were taken out of the capital for safe storage, the empty galleries were used for free public concerts. Beata was able to attend the performances by the celebrated pianist Myra Hess who gave a continuous series of piano concerts from 1939 to 1946, including programs of 'German music'. German culture was not rejected in Britain during the war's duration as it had been during the 1914-18 War.

Information and correspondence from their family ceased after 1942. Their anxieties continued and multiplied throughout the War until its end when Beata and Tom were able to start the search for them in the chaos of post-war Europe, principally through the Red Cross.

The shock of what they eventually discovered marked them both for the rest of their lives. The last poems of *Breaking Glass* are an account of the end of the war and a personal reckoning, the traumatic loss of their mother and the problems in their relationship with their father, Hans, whom they held responsible for the collapse of their parents' marriage.

While Hans had been interned on the Isle Of Man in 1940, he produced a notable contemporary version of Shakespeare's Julius Caesar in the internment camp. After his release, he went on to work with scripts, plays and government propaganda in London and for the US forces in France during the last years of the war. He was also politically active, founding with other refugees in London the 'Club 43', to research and publish essays on the future of Germany after the War. With his second wife he emigrated to New York in 1946 to teach drama at the New School for Social Research (with the playwright Tennessee Williams as one of his students), assisted by his old friend the director Irwen Piscator and his theatre associate, the playwright Bertolt Brecht. He found it difficult to establish a new career in the US and returned to Germany in 1950, first living in Hamburg and then Munich, returning to a German cultural world and practice in the German language. With a renewed career in both West and East Germany he continued with scripts, plays and novels, receiving an award from the first post-war West German Chancellor Konrad Adenauer. He served as President of the Society of Script Writers and his collected literary works were published by Rutten & Loening, Berlin in 1967.

Tom had further studied and lectured throughout the War while working for the war effort. He was elected as a member of the Institution of Electrical Engineers and finally emigrated to the United States of America in 1958, receiving his Doctorate from Imperial College, London in 1960. He continued to practise as an electronics engineer and research scientist with the many electronic companies of the Boston area and was a visiting lecturer at MIT.

Explanatory Notes to the Poetry

11 *Beata!*
The attempt by refugees to anglicise their German names, to make them easier for the English ear or change them altogether for the English equivalent, was the subject of much comedy. In this case, Beata changes one letter.

13 *Other People's Houses*
The opening quote was I believe made by the parents of a child refugee placed on one of the Kindertransports from Germany in the 1930s, the quote in the poem by a fellow refugee.

21 *Strindberg's Grandson*
A descendant of the playwright Strindberg was a fellow pupil at the Bunce Court School and became close to Beata, though Essinger the headmistress had discouraged romantic relationships. *Miss Julie, The Father* and *The Dream Play* are of course the titles to Strindberg's major plays.

22 *The Death of Ophelia*
The daughter of the actor Robertson Hare became a friend of Beata at her next school. Her father Hans would have been pleased with this contact for Beata's sake as well as his own ambitions in the London theatre.

25 *Cable Street*
Cable Street was the central location in Whitechapel, the East End of London, of several demonstrations and street battles in 1936 between Oswald Mosley's 'Blackshirts' of the British Union of Fascists, the Police, and the local Jewish population, supported by the Irish and other communities and socialist groups.

27 & 29 *The Moon Coin, Athene's Song*
After 1934 Beata and Tom kept in direct contact with their family still in Germany until 1939, thereafter by post via relatives in the USA. This would include letters from their grandfather Eugen Rehfisch, supporting their mother Lilli until his death in 1937.

30 *The Hill*
A reference to the Haverstock Hill in Belsize Park and its shops and cafes. Reminiscent of the 'continental café' there were several cafes, including Cosmo, frequented by the refugee community. There were many well-known members of this community, including Sigmund Freud, and a remarkable group of young artists and writers including the poet Erich Fried, a personal friend of Beata, who went on to establish a prestigious literary career in post-war Germany and Austria.

32 *Troikas*
After learning to touch-type Beata worked voluntarily for the Central Office For Refugees at Bloomsbury House (the former Palace Hotel in Bloomsbury Street, London), an organisation set up to assist refugees to the UK. This intensive work included: the entry visas and substantial sureties required by the British Government, particularly with the large number of applicants after 1938; organising host families across Britain; the welfare of children from the Kindertransport trains, and the welfare and release of internees after June 1940 from the internment camps of the Isle Of Man.

35 *My Wolves*
London Zoo in nearby Regent's Park was kept open throughout the War. Valuable animals were evacuated to locations outside London, leaving behind other animals such as the collection of wolves. The crown of the Primrose Hill (between Regent's Park and Belsize Park) was the location of anti-aircraft guns to protect the nearby railway lines vulnerable

to bombing (featured by the poet Louis MacNeice in his 'Autumn Journal').

36 To Be Important, The Philosopher, The Physicist
These poems express the intensely personal experiences of Beata and her friends, perhaps in response to the threat and tension of the War. The 'philosopher' went on to teach in universities in the UK; the 'physicist' became eminent in his profession.

37 'Potato Pete'
The personas of 'Captain Carrot' and 'Potato Pete' were creations of the Ministry of Agriculture, with advertisement campaigns to encourage the consumption of crops readily grown in the British Isles, part of the 'Dig For Victory' campaign.

45 The Offcuts
Among many jobs Beata worked with several local 'cottage industries', including the one she describes, using offcuts of materials (wood and metal) recycled from industry to make toys, kitchen gadgets, small furniture etc. Her employment in these workshops was often with fellow refugees and neighbours in their own homes and gardens. The style connection made to the radical design school, the Bauhaus in Germany (closed in 1933), is an ironic interpretation of these geometric offcuts.

48 'Tyrannos'
Newsreel films were featured at many cinemas and were the means for the government to relay the progress of the war. 'In Tyrannos' was the title of an essay on the subject of tyranny by her father Hans Rehfisch and published as part of his activities with the 'Club 43'. He wrote scripts and propaganda for the BBC and the US forces.

49, 51 & 61 *Goethe, Beethoven, Abschied*

In contrast to World War I there seems to have been less popular anti-German sentiment during World War II, this second conflict described as with 'the Nazis' as much as with Germany. German culture, her literature and music, was still enjoyed by the British public, including the popular concerts at London's National Gallery given by Myra Hess of piano music by German composers throughout the War. The National Gallery in Trafalgar Square was close to Charing Cross Railway Station, an embarkation station for the troops for Europe.

53 *Top-Secret*

After he had left the Bunce Court School Beata's brother Tom had quickly qualified, working his way through training and education from the early age of sixteen in mathematics and engineering and by 1940 was employed on research of 'government importance' and not interned. His research employment included the Murphy Radio Company and the production of military radios and large valves for the first commercial domestic televisions. Tom was interviewed by Robert Watson-Watt, the scientist leading the urgent development of radar for military use who needed large valves for radar instruments. Tom went on with further research throughout the War with the Electrical Research Association (ERA), set up by the Government to coordinate these areas of war-time research and development and would have been bound by the Official Secrets Act.

56 *Fireworks*

The public bomb shelters, including the Underground train stations, were usually crowded and Tom and Beata turned to their back garden 'Anderson' shelter or slept with a mattress under the kitchen table in their flat during the air-raids of the Blitz. I understand Tom, Hans and Beata all took turns to volunteer for fire-watching during the raids; broken sleep seems to have been a common condition of their wartime lives.

60 *Breaking Glass*

Arthur Miller's late play *Broken Glass* focuses on the relationship between a woman who has a mysterious paralysis and her controlling husband, associating her paralysis with the destructive events of Kristallnacht of 1938 in Germany. Beata was possibly stimulated by the play, at the London staging in 2011, to create her own image of 'breaking glass' and its symbolic potential.

64 & 66 *A Bitterness of Temper, Milk*

Beata's father, Hans Rehfisch, initially trained as a lawyer but after military service in World War I he launched a successful career as a playwright and scriptwriter in Germany, often writing with a series of pen names. On his arrival in London he continued with scripts and plays, writing in English, as well as propaganda and broadcasts.

Despite efforts by both Tom and Beata to get their mother a visa, Lilli remained in Berlin until it was too late to emigrate with the advent of World War II. Their fears as to her fate were to be confirmed after the war had ended, and both felt that their father had been responsible for a lack of will in her emigration from Germany, during the years of the couple's protracted divorce.

67 *Summer Sonata*

With Beethoven's Sonata 110 this poem echoes the poem *Für Elise* of *Berlin Blues* with the power of music to transcend. The playing of the piano seems to have worked as a memory-aide for Beata, an evocation through sound of her Berlin family, particularly her mother, and the world of music they had created and enjoyed in her childhood.

69 *What Happened to the Toys?*

The distinct character of German toys and their symbolism, and in this poem what had been 'left behind', is also the theme of *The Doll's House* poem of *Berlin Blues*.

70 *Starving Myself*

After the outbreak of the War in 1939, Tom and Beata were able to continue to receive and send letters to their mother in Berlin (and other family members remaining in Germany) via distant relatives in the neutral USA, up to Lilli's arrest and deportation in 1941. How much they knew of her privations and how much she wanted to tell them was an understood correspondence of omission.

71 *Gin*

The 'Duties' would have referred to the public expectations of volunteering with tasks such as fire-watching, helping with relief stations, caring for children and the elderly.

Music Halls or Variety Halls (as with the cinema) were still kept open to the public throughout the War. A.P.Herbert was a soldier and politician who served as an MP during the War, he was also a humorist and wrote revues with lyrics including this quote.

Acknowledgements

I want to thank the publisher and editor Siobhan Harrison of the Writesideleft Press for her energy, enthusiasm and editorial critique for this collection. I also want to thank all who have continued to encourage and advise me during the long journey in putting together this collection, including the many poets who knew Beata and her poetry: Anne Berkley, Alan Brownjohn, Jennifer Grigg, Sue Hubbard, Jane Kirwan, Christopher Reid, Maurice Riordan, Julian Stannard, Sara Wardle, Hugo Williams and Mary Woodward.

I would also thank my family again, Robert, Ifor, Gabriella and Marilyn for their research and critique, moral support and belief in the continued publication of Beata's work.

Stephen Duncan September 2019

WriteSideLeft
2019

www.writesideleft.com